Introduction

Few subjects have created more disturbance in the Body of Christ than the issue of the eternal security of the believer. Simply stated, this is the question:

Can a Christian ever lose his/her salvation? Amplified, the larger question would be:

Once a person has been born again into the family of God—received new life, a new nature, been justified and sealed by the Holy Spirit—can that individual ever become *unsaved* by sinning, or by ceasing to believe, or by any other cause?

In our fast-paced world of empty words, carnality, and shallow faith, not to mention the growing number of religious charlatans and defectors, the question becomes all the more important.

This booklet is a brief yet potent statement worth your serious consideration. Because of its size, some things had to be omitted . . . but none of the vital ingredients of the issue are missing. In clear, uncomplicated terms, a doctrine that has been twisted and abused is explained so that anyone can understand. Free from ridiculous, unbalanced extremes, these words offer you a reassuring, calm, and quiet confidence that you are absolutely secure in the everlasting arms of your eternal Savior. In Him you are safe!

In fact, that is the *only* place you can be perfectly safe today.

Charles R. Swindoll

Eternal Security

Lucy and Linus, now famous little people in Charles Schulz's cartoon *Peanuts*, are staring out the window. The rain is pouring down.

Lucy speaks: "Boy, look at it rain . . . what if it floods the whole world?"

Linus answers: "It will never do that. In the ninth chapter of Genesis, God promised Noah that would never happen again, and the sign of the promise is the rainbow."

Lucy is looking directly at him as he is speaking. She turns back toward the window, smiles big, and announces: "You've taken a great load off my mind."

To which Linus responds: "Sound theology has a way of doing that!"

Wise and timely words from little Linus. With feelings of fear and uncertainty while watching events from our windows, many of us often hear least what we need most. Sound, reliable theology that offers reassurance and hope . . . based squarely on God's Word, the Bible. Not feelings or opinions or even logic. We need to hear what God has said and rest our case there.

As we think through the issues of the eternal security of the believer, our desire is to let God speak to us from the Scriptures. In doing so, most of our questions will be answered and our struggles will begin to cease. But at the outset, let me encourage you to set aside all your defenses and relax your grip on any preconceived notions. To borrow from Lucy's response to Linus, God is ready to "take a great load off your mind" if you will simply accept what He declares.

Three Crucial Factors about Salvation

As I ponder this subject, there are three crucial factors that impact the question: Can a Christian ever lose his/her salvation?

1. We have in mind an individual who is truly born again. One who possesses eternal life through faith in God's Son, the Lord Jesus Christ. Possessors, not professors.

Nowhere in Scripture does God promise eternal life to people who have done religious things, but have never truly accepted the gift of eternal life, having changed their minds from the rejection of Christ to faith in Him. No hand raising, no walking down an aisle, no prayer, no church membership or baptism or sacrificial act or giving of money or attending evangelistic crusades will ever take the place of being born again. People who actually possess eternal life are directly linked by faith to Jesus, the Christ. Personally and deliberately, they have believed that Jesus died and rose from the dead for them.

Listen to the truth:

*And the witness is this, that God has
given us eternal life, and this life is in
His Son.*

*He who has the Son has the life; he
who does not have the Son of God does
not have the life (1 John 5:11-12).*

*He saved us, not on the basis of deeds
which we have done in righteousness,
but according to His mercy, by the
washing of regeneration and renewing
by the Holy Spirit,*

*whom He poured out upon us richly
through Jesus Christ our Savior, that
being justified by His grace we might be
made heirs according to the hope of
eternal life (Titus 3:5-7).*

*For by grace you have been saved
through faith; and that not of yourselves,
it is the gift of God;*

*not as a result of works, that no one
should boast (Ephesians 2:8-9).*

Familiar words, but seldom taken *literally.*
The person we are considering in this booklet is
truly and absolutely a child of God.

2. The subject is eternal se-
curity, not temporal carnality. We are not deal-
ing with God's disciplining His wayward children.

If you mix these two subjects, you'll be hope-
lessly confused. Carnality has to do with the believer who willfully walks in the flesh and
chooses a lifestyle that lacks the power and control of the Holy Spirit. If you will pause long
enough to read three New Testament passages
(1 Corinthians 3:1-3; Galatians 5:16-23; He-

brews 12:5-13), you'll see that a carnal Christian is a child of God who lives under the discipline of the Lord. Those scriptures do not refer to a Christian who has lost his salvation, but rather one who has become wayward, one who is walking in the energy of the flesh.

Interestingly, those who teach that a Christian is not eternally secure usually have no place in their theology for carnality—and yet the Scriptures clearly set forth the sad but real fact that a child of God can slump into periods of carnality. But as is true of children in our own family, they are still our children even if they willfully disobey us. We discipline them, but we cannot ever say they are not our children. Don't confuse eternal security with temporary carnality.

3. We must focus on what God has done for His children, not what we have done for Him. This is foundational. Salvation is not something we earn, but rather something we receive as a gift. We did not pursue God, He pursued us. He came to our rescue when we were without righteousness, without a shred of hope.

But God demonstrates His own love toward us, in that while we were yet sinners, Christ died for us (Romans 5:8).

And you were dead in your trespasses and sins,

in which you formerly walked according to the course of this world, according to the prince of the power of the air, of the spirit that is now working in the sons of disobedience.

Among them we too all formerly lived in the lusts of our flesh, indulging the

desires of the flesh and of the mind, and
were by nature children of wrath, even
as the rest.

But God, being rich in mercy, because
of His great love with which He loved
us,

even when we were dead in our trans-
gressions, made us alive together with
Christ (by grace you have been saved),

and raised us up with Him, and
seated us with Him in the heavenly
places, in Christ Jesus,

in order that in the ages to come He
might show the surpassing riches of His
grace in kindness toward us in Christ
Jesus (Ephesians 2:1-7).

When did our salvation occur? Look again at
Romans 5:8—"while we were yet sinners." And,
according to Ephesians 2, when we were spiritu-
ally "dead." When "we were by nature children of
wrath."

Without wanting to be overbearing, I believe
this must be the starting point for an under-
standing of eternal security. Since salvation is
not something we earn or win, since it is not
something we ourselves achieved, then it stands
to reason that we ourselves cannot take it away.
Salvation is God's gift. It is His power that makes
it possible . . . and it is unthinkable and impossible for you and me to alter in any way the ulti-
mate accomplishment of His plan.

Question: Can the Work of God Be Undone?

Please consider the follow-
ing statement very carefully. I'd like you to read it
twice. The first time slowly, to yourself. The sec-

ond time aloud.

**Since my security depends on what God
has done for me through Christ, then
various works of God would have to be
undone or reversed if I could lose my
salvation . . . and the Bible would
certainly declare it.**

Before reading any further, *do you agree with
that?* Perhaps a little analysis would help. First,
it's clear from the Scriptures that our salvation
has been made possible through Christ's work
on the cross, not our human effort. God offers
mankind eternal life as a gift, not as a reward,
right? Second, if it were possible for me to lose
my salvation, then God would have to reverse the
transaction in some way, i.e., take back His gift
or somehow strip me of His forgiveness, what-
ever. Then third, His Word would make that very
clear so all of us could be adequately warned.

You see, if we start with God—as we certainly
should—then we must say that He takes back
the gift He said was ours, when we say we have
lost our salvation. On top of that, the Bible would
definitely include verses that explicitly state
such facts.

Not only is it unthinkable that God would take
back an eternal promise, it is impossible. Remember, He is immutable. That means He is un-
changing. He cannot lie. Nor does He ever state
that the gift of eternal life is on loan to us . . . on
the contrary, Hebrews 10:14 clearly declares:

*For by one offering He has perfected
for all time those who are sanctified.*

The "one offering" refers to Christ's sacrificial
death on the cross. And the result? We are told

that "He has perfected *for all time* those who are sanctified" (emphasis mine). When we believe, when we take the gift of eternal life, we are set apart unto God, distinctly and uniquely His (sanctified), just as a new baby born into your home is set apart unto you. And God says it is a transaction that is in effect "for all time." No, there is nothing temporary in this arrangement.

You see, all the value of the finished work of Christ is placed by God to the credit of the sinner. Nothing can alter this. It is "for all time." Therefore, to suggest that the Christian's eternal acceptance is dependent upon his own conduct from one day to the next is really a slur upon the finished work of Christ. Actually, what that says is that Christ only *began* the work, you and I must finish it. And if that were so, then we would deserve some of the glory. Nothing could be further from the truth.

Scriptures Emphasizing God's Secure Hold on the Believer

Within the New Testament there are several passages worth consideration. Let's give attention to them for the next few minutes. Listen to 1 Corinthians 12:13:

For by one Spirit we were all baptized into one body, whether Jews or Greeks, whether slaves or free, and we were all made to drink of one Spirit.

The Christian is said to be in the body, no matter his/her race or rank, and in full possession of the Spirit. If we could lose our salvation, we would certainly be expelled from the body. And yet no such idea is even hinted at in all the Bible. Not a single verse states that one who was once "in Christ" is now "out of Christ." This brings us to a promise Jesus gave while He was on earth:

"All that the Father gives Me shall come to Me, and the one who comes to Me I will certainly not cast out" (John 6:37).

Just in case you are still struggling with the idea that salvation rests with God, not us, please observe that Jesus says it is the Father who gives us to the Son. Equally important, don't miss the fact that Jesus Himself stated that "the one who comes to Me I will certainly not cast out."

The Greek text declares a double negative—a highly emphatic statement that might be paraphrased "the one who comes to me I will positively and absolutely *not* throw out." No "ifs," "ands," "buts," or "howevers" about it. This does not mean merely "I will not reject or refuse," but also "I will not give up after receiving." Nothing temporary about that!

Now, consider Ephesians 1:13 and 4:30:

In Him, you also, after listening to the message of truth, the gospel of your salvation—having also believed, you were sealed in Him with the Holy Spirit of promise.

And do not grieve the Holy Spirit of God, by whom you were sealed for the day of redemption.

Not only does the Holy Spirit place us into the universal Body of Christ, He "seals" us. This seal goes into effect from the moment we believe. If we could lose our salvation, obviously that seal would have to be broken. But that would contradict God's promise. If He says we are sealed for the day of redemption (the day we receive new bodies that will last forever), then we can be certain nothing will interrupt that divine plan. Neither here nor anywhere else do the Scriptures speak of the Spirit's seal being broken—or loosened.

Romans 8:1 is also worth our attention:

There is therefore now no condemnation for those who are in Christ Jesus.

And with that verse, Romans 8:31-39:

What then shall we say to these things? If God is for us, who is against us?

He who did not spare His own Son, but delivered Him up for us all, how will He not also with Him freely give us all things?

Who will bring a charge against God's elect? God is the one who justifies;

who is the one who condemns? Christ Jesus is He who died, yes, rather who was raised, who is at the right hand of God, who also intercedes for us.

Who shall separate us from the love of Christ? Shall tribulation, or distress, or persecution, or famine, or nakedness, or peril, or sword?

Just as it is written,

"FOR THY SAKE WE ARE BEING PUT TO DEATH ALL DAY LONG; WE WERE CONSIDERED AS SHEEP TO BE SLAUGHTERED."

But in all these things we

*overwhelmingly conquer through Him
who loved us.*

*For I am convinced that neither death,
nor life, nor angels, nor principalities,
nor things present, nor things to come,
nor powers,*

*nor height, nor depth, nor any other
created thing, shall be able to separate
us from the love of God, which is in Christ
Jesus our Lord.*

The strongest possible term for eternal punishment is translated "condemnation" in Romans 8:1. We are assured that we do not face such punishment once we are "in Christ Jesus." And the last section of Romans 8 further assures us that we have God on our side!

Who will bring a charge against us? There is no accuser!

Who will condemn us? There is no judge!

Who will separate us from the love of Christ? There is no executioner!

Why? Because we are secure in Christ Jesus. And if you look closely, you will see that none of these promises are *conditional.* God is for us (v. 31). We overwhelmingly conquer (v. 37). We are enveloped, protected, safe, and secure against *all* possible threats (vv. 38-39).

And our study of Scripture would be incomplete if we failed to examine John 10:27-29:

*"My sheep hear My voice, and I know
them, and they follow Me;*

*and I give eternal life to them, and
they shall never perish; and no one shall
snatch them out of my hand.*

"My Father, who has given them to Me, is greater than all; and no one is able to snatch them out of the Father's hand."

Read those words with discernment. Of whom is Jesus speaking? They are His followers. Christians. True believers. Now, these verses do not talk about how a person *becomes* a sheep, but rather the results of *being* a sheep. Jesus is explaining that it is the Father's purpose to keep us secure in spite of everything and everyone!

Look closely. We are surrounded by a *double* wall of security. We are in Christ's eternal grip and "no one shall snatch them" out of Jesus' hand. And then He, in turn, states that we and He are in the Father's hand, making it absolutely impossible for anyone to be able "to snatch them out of the Father's hand."

Listen to 1 John 5:18b:

. . . He who was born of God keeps him and the evil one does not touch him.

See the word "touch." One reliable authority says that the original Greek term means "to assault, in order to sever the vital union between Christ and the believer."[1] Not even the devil with all his supernatural power can assault the believer so as to sever our eternal union. Magnificent promise! Those who are born again are "kept" by Christ.

One final verse is deserving of our attention —the next-to-the-last verse in the letter of Jude:

Now to Him who is able to keep you from stumbling, and to make you stand in the presence of His glory blameless with great joy . . ." (Jude 24).

The scene is that future day when the believer stands before Christ prior to his/her entering into the glory of heaven. How shall we stand? Ashamed? Uncertain of our entrance? Insecure and seized by fear? No way! We are promised that He is the One who will make us stand "in the presence of his glory blameless with great joy." Blameless!

We have examined one scripture after another that carries the same theme. We have learned that our salvation really rests on God's strength, not ours. And that our safety is in Christ's power, not ours. And that our protection depends on the Father's firm grip, not ours. And that no one, including the devil, can sever the vital union that connects us with the Lord Jesus Christ. Why? Because it was His death and resurrection that perfected us "for all time" . . . because of His finished work, not ours.

Why Some Doubt and Deny

As we trace our way through these many passages (there are dozens more), you might begin to wonder how anyone could ever doubt and deny that the Christian is secure. Having spoken with some who struggle with this doctrine, I have discovered that most of them have difficulty in four areas: certain problem passages, fear that this will lead to loose living, a misunderstanding of carnality, and feelings of unworthiness. These deserve an answer.

Problem Passages

Admittedly, there are certain scriptures that seem, at first glance, to teach that Christians can drift so far from God that they are no longer in His family. Rather than taking the time to examine those few verses, let me give you some guidelines to follow when you encounter such verses.

1. Read the words of the verse *very* carefully.

2. Study the "setting" or context of the verse.

3. Remember that God cannot contradict Himself. He certainly would not be saying one thing here and another thing elsewhere.

4. Pray for wisdom and insight.

5. Seek the counsel of resources—either reliable books or careful students of the Scriptures you admire. But mainly compare scripture with scripture.

6. If you still cannot understand, patiently wait for God to show you in days to come. His Word is like a deep, deep mine, and some of its riches do not fall into our laps at the snap of our fingers.

Fear of Loose Living

Romans 6:1-11 declares a serious warning. Take the time to read these words:

Well then, shall we keep on sinning so that God can keep on showing us more and more kindness and forgiveness?
Of course not! Should we keep on sinning when we don't have to? For sin's power over us was broken when we became Christians and were baptized

to become a part of Jesus Christ; through
his death the power of your sinful nature
was shattered. Your old sin-loving
nature was buried with him by baptism
when he died, and when God the
Father, with glorious power, brought
him back to life again, you were given
his wonderful new life to enjoy.

For you have become a part of him,
and so you died with him, so to speak,
when he died; and now you share his
new life, and shall rise as he did. Your
old evil desires were nailed to the cross
with him; that part of you that loves to
sin was crushed and fatally wounded,
so that your sin-loving body is no longer
under sin's control, no longer needs to
be a slave to sin; for when you are
deadened to sin you are freed from all
its allure and its power over you. And
since your old sin-loving nature "died"
with Christ, we know that you will share
his new life. Christ rose from the dead
and will never die again. Death no
longer has any power over him. He died
once for all to end sin's power, but now
he lives forever in unbroken fellowship
with God. So look upon your old sin
nature as dead and unresponsive to sin,
and instead be alive to God, alert to him,
through Jesus Christ our Lord (TLB).

Any doctrine can be abused . . . but that is
hardly a reason to reject that doctrine! It is my
personal conviction that a firm, calm belief in
eternal security provides a greater motivation to

live for Christ than fear of losing my salvation. Quite frankly, if the latter were true, all that would be necessary to rectify my problem would be to get saved again. And again. And again.

You see, if I know that I am secure in the Father's hand—and that my loose living would be met with His strong discipline, the impetus to walk in the light would be there at all times! Ask any Christian who has spent much time under the smarting rod of God. It is *anything* but pleasant.

Misunderstanding of Carnality

As I mentioned earlier, those who hold to an insecure salvation leave little room in their teaching for carnality. And yet the New Testament is replete with illustrations of believers who drifted away from the Lord. That is the whole point of the prodigal son (Luke 15:11-24). The boy truly deserved to be cast out—but he wasn't. The father could have rejected the son—but he didn't.

Unpleasant though it may be, carnality *is* an option. It bears grave and grim consequences, but we are not to confuse it with a loss of salvation. According to 1 Corinthians 11:30-32, there were some believers in ancient Corinth who continued to live such carnal lives, God removed them from the earth . . . and yet even *that* discipline is not to be confused with condemnation.

For this reason many among you are weak and sick, and a number sleep.
But if we judged ourselves rightly, we should not be judged.
But when we are judged, we are disciplined by the Lord in order that we

*may not be condemned along with the
world.*

Remember, we who have believed in Christ will
never, ever be condemned (Romans 8:1).

Feelings of Unworthiness

If we adopted a human logic,
this would be a very natural problem. But all the
way through this booklet we have resisted the
human perspective. We have refused to rely on
feelings or turn to logic for our answers.

Some days I do not "feel" married. But I am.
There are days I do not "feel" like I am almost fifty
years old. But I am. And there are times I don't
"feel" worthy of my family's love. But it is there in
abundance. My feelings are often terribly unreli-
able. So are yours.

Remember the prodigal? After he came to his
senses he returned to his dad and began his
speech in all sincerity.

*"And the son said to him, 'Father, I
have sinned against heaven and in your
sight; I am no longer worthy to be called
your son' "* (Luke 15:21).

But his faithful, gracious, forgiving, patient father interrupted that speech with sweeping ac-
tions of mercy and grace. He restored the worth-
less, undeserving, once-rebellious son to a place
of significance in the family. Without reserva-
tion, the father hugged his son home . . . the
same son who "felt" so unworthy.

Guilt does an awful number on us. It will lie to
us and beat us into submission. It will convince
us that God's promises really don't apply to us. It
will yell so loudly we will mistake it for the voice of

God. It will put us down, stomp on us, remove us from circulation, and push us so far under that we will begin to question our own sanity.

But the beauty of grace (our only permanent deliverance from guilt) is that it meets us where we are and gives us what we don't deserve.

I acknowledged my sin to Thee,
And my iniquity I did not hide;
I said, "I will confess my transgressions
to the LORD";
And Thou didst forgive the guilt of my sin
(Psalm 32:5).

Guilty child of God, look up. Refuse to let your guilt convince you of a lie. You are God's child if you have been born into His family. You do not need to be born again, again! You need to "acknowledge" your sinful way. You need to "confess the transgressions" of your life to your Lord. On the authority of His Word, I assure you that He will forgive your sin *and* remove the accompanying guilt.

Do that now!

An Old Testament Example

Tucked away in the first book of the Bible is a remarkable story. It illustrates the truth of all that we've been thinking about in this booklet. It's the age-old story of the flood in the days of Noah.

But rather than focusing our attention upon the forty days and nights of rain or the universal scope of the deluge, let's think about those eight people who were preserved from death. According to Genesis 7:7-10, Mr. and Mrs. Noah, plus their three sons and their sons' wives, along with the animals, entered the ark before the water of the flood began to rise upon the earth.

Those who have an eye for detail do not overlook a very significant part of the account. As the biblical record reveals the events that transpired just before the flood, the inspired writer makes a notation that is extremely important:

> *So they went into the ark to Noah, by twos of all flesh in which was the breath of life.*
>
> *And those that entered, male and female of all flesh, entered as God had commanded him; and the LORD closed it behind him.*
>
> *Then the flood came upon the earth for forty days; and the water increased and lifted up the ark, so that it rose above the earth.*
>
> *And the water prevailed and increased greatly upon the earth; and the ark floated on the surface of the water* (Genesis 7:15-18).

Did you catch the comment? We read that as soon as the animals and Noah with his family were in the ark as God had commanded, ". . . the Lord closed it behind him." Who closed the door? *The Lord.* Who is responsible for the security of all those lives? *The Lord.* He personally saw to it that the righteous were safely locked inside.

The fountains of the great deep burst open and the floodgates of the sky split apart as never before or since in the history of time. We cannot imagine the incredible scene of disaster that blasted the earth all around that tiny floating barge. But inside—removed from danger—there

was divine security. The brevity of words high-
lights the magnificent keeping power of Al-
mighty God.

> . . . and only Noah was left, together
> with those that were with him in the ark
> (Genesis 7:23b).

No anxiety ate at them. No fear that somehow
they might sink. No sleepless nights, wondering
if disaster would soon interrupt their peace and
safety. No, we do not find a word in the record of
any such thing. Why? Because *the Lord had
closed them in.* Their security rested in His
strength, not theirs. So we aren't surprised to
read these words following the flood:

> *So Noah went out, and his sons and
> his wife and his sons' wives with him.*
> *Every beast, every creeping thing, and
> every bird, everything that moves on the
> earth, went out by their families from the
> ark* (Genesis 8:18-19).

The One who had closed them in and preserved them through the disaster, finally re-
leased them into an entirely new world, a fresh
beginning.

And that is exactly what He plans to do with
us. The One who closed us in at the moment of
our new birth is currently preserving us from
any and all threats . . . and will some day release
us into His eternal home. Blameless!

Concluding Comfort

With a sensitive eye on God's
Word throughout this booklet, I have forged out
my belief in the eternal security of the Christian.
I find that this doctrine weaves its way peacefully

and perfectly through the fabric of God's Word. Also, I find that the alternative position leaves little (if any) room for the large amount of teaching in the New Testament on the carnal Christian.

Candidly, if I did not believe that my salvation was eternally and permanently secure, I would be living my entire life without confidence and inner peace. I would forever wonder, "How far is *too* far?" In other words, if my salvation could be lost, I would never know if I had drifted too far. And this would leave me in such a state of uneasiness that I seriously doubt if I could live one day free of worry. And I mean *serious* anxiety.

But being absolutely confident and comforted in the fact that my salvation is secure, based on God's keeping power, not mine, all cause for anxiety is removed. I may tremble on the Rock, but the Rock never trembles under me! And that inner assurance not only relieves my fear, it allows me to carry on with much greater efficiency. And rather than causing me to be indifferent and irresponsible, it inspires me to direct all my energies toward those things that please and glorify the name of my heavenly Father . . . eternally protected because He has me in His all-powerful hand.

In 1937 the famous Golden Gate bridge was completed. At that time it was the world's longest suspension bridge. The entire project cost the United States Government $77,000,000. During the process of constructing the first section of the bridge, very few safety devices were used, resulting in twenty-three accidental deaths as workers fell helplessly into the waters far below.

The toll was so significant, something had to be done before the second section was built. An ingenious plan was arranged. The largest safety net in the world (it alone cost $100,000!) was made out of stout manila cordage and stretched out beneath the work crews. It proved to be an excellent investment in view of the fact that it saved the lives of at least ten men who fell into it without injury. Furthermore, the work went twenty-five percent faster, since the workers were relieved from the fear of falling to their deaths.

God's great net of security spans this globe. No matter where His children live, He has stretched out beneath them His everlasting arms. As a result, every one of us can live and work freely and fearlessly, knowing that we are protected, safe, secure, sealed, and kept by Him.

The anxiety and fear of perishing are gone. Eternal security has taken that great load off our minds.

As Linus once said, "Sound theology has a way of doing that."

Faithful God of grace:

Your Word is such a source of comfort. In a calm, clear manner it has spoken, leaving us encouraged.

Thank you for replacing fear with confidence. And for removing ignorance with reliable information we needed to know. Thank you for sound theology!

Insecurity abounds. We don't know what tomorrow holds. We have no absolute assurance that we'll be employed. Or have our health. Or enjoy the presence of family and friends. Our lives are like a puff of smoke, as uncertain as the morning fog.

But one thing is for sure. Being in Christ is the safest place in life. And in calamity. And in death. In Him, and in Him alone, we are secure. Eternally secure.

And we are eternally grateful . . . through Christ our Lord.

Amen.

[1]W. E. Vine, *An Expository Dictionary of New Testament Words*, Vol. 4 (Westwood, N. J.: Fleming H. Revell Company, 1940), p. 145.